David Steinberg

W Allen

Tony Danza

Vanity

Tom Berenger

Nolan Miller

Lauren Hutton

**Portrait HOLLYWOOD**

For Dave
Warm Wishes

[signature] '96

# PORT

# HOLLY

GARY BERNSTEIN'S CLASSIC

FOREWORD B

WOODFORD • PRESS

# RAIT WOOD

## CELEBRITY PHOTOGRAPHS

ELIZABETH TAYLOR

SAN • FRANCISCO

**Published by**
**Woodford Press**
660 Market Street
San Francisco, California 94104

Book Design: Laurence J. Hyman
Editor: Jon Rochmis

## ACKNOWLEDGMENTS

To Iris and Art for your love and for life—I miss you both dearly. To Doris Lane for taking over and being the ultimate survival role-model. To Don and Gerry Levitt for always being there. I'm grateful for your trust and love . . . and Donnie, I'll always appreciate the sailor cap. To Hans Prauser, for the original inspiration, your friendship . . . and even the locusts. To Bill Coleman for expanding my vision. To Dick Davies, for your confidence at the very start. To Max Evans, for taking a chance on a young shooter. To John McMurray for your loving friendship and all the great times. To Aldo Cipullo, for your talent, the laughs and for the jingle bell (Max, John, Aldo, I miss you all). To Jean-Paul Germain for your chic and of course Acapulco. To Manny Mercado, muchas gracias mi amigo. To Mirella Forlani for your love and friendship. To John Shirilla and Marc Sirken—you guys are the real bwanas. To Robb Carr and Jim Crocker, for the hundreds of images you viewed with my eyes. To Bob Goldstein, Cindy Edelson, Julie Grosse and Joe Notaro for bringing me into the computer era with such sensitivity and talent. To Denny Bond, for the years we tried to mix peanut butter with tuna fish (but most of all for the Botticelli). To Rick Hustead for the innumerable times you fouled me in the low post, and for your years of honorable dedication and friendship; you've been a brother. To Dan Frank for being "family," and for always coming to our rescue—you are the best. To Cheń Sam for a world of energy, support and fun. To Judy-Judy-Judy Bryer with love and appreciation. To Robert Cavallo for keeping me legal and legit (well, almost). To my only Masters, Ron Scanlon and Ben Smith, for showing me the way to personal strength and inner peace. To Robert Wagner for your support, friendship and some pretty amazing jokes. I owe you a lot, R.J. To Mike Emerson for your artistry and vision. To Bill Gladstone and Laurence Hyman, for being my brothers in vision and spirit from the gate. And to B.J. Sutton, the kindest man I've ever known, and most certainly the one who has given me the greatest gift of all.

DEDICATION: To my wonderful daughters, Romé and Caron. I love you with all my heart. Daddy.

A Tara Rose book

Based on an original concept by Michael S. Emerson and Nancy Gaelen
Production coordination: Michael S. Emerson
Digital imaging: ZZYZX Visual Systems, Hollywood, California
Color separations: Riverside Scans, West Sacramento, California
Printed in Hong Kong

ISBN: 0-942627-02-4

Library of Congress Card Catalog Number: 94-60747

# CONTENTS

Jay Acovone, 103

Maud Adams, 60

Nancy Allen, 16

Peter Allen, 9

Herb Alpert, 80

Paul Anka, 110

Christopher Atkins, 30

Catherine Bach, 25

Stephanie Beacham, 146

Tom Berenger, 120

Corbin Bernsen, 54

Troy Beyer, 126

Sonny Bono, 44

David Brenner, 59

Charlie Brill, 52

James Brolin, 58

Dyan Cannon, 39, 112

Truman Capote, 115

Diahann Carroll, 119

Johnny Carson, E, F, G, 113

Chevy Chase, 31

Cher, 44

Rae Dawn Chong, 85

James Coburn, 132

Natalie Cole, 47

Joan Collins, 4, 32, 101, 123

Tony Danza, 88

John Davidson, 106

Pam Dawber, 29

Patrick Duffy, 150

Robert Duvall, 2

Linda Evans, 136, 137

Farrah Fawcett, 153

Peter Fonda, 83

John Forsythe, 102

Mary Frann, 107

Eva Gabor, 93, 94

Leeza Gibbons, 73

Frank Gifford, 131

Kathie Lee Gifford, 131

Alexander Godunov, 99

Elliott Gould, 40

Stewart Granger, 109

Kehly Gray, 72

Linda Gray, 27, 72

Lorne Greene, 71

David Allen Grier, 91

Larry Hagman, 8

Uva Harden, 38

Neil Patrick Harris, 69

Katherine Helmond, 43

Margaux Hemingway, 38

Doug Henning, 84

Charlton Heston, 61

Christopher Hewitt, 66

Anna Maria Hordesford, 67

Lee Horsley, 74

Rock Hudson, A, B, C, D,148

Lauren Hutton, 10

Kathy Ireland, 151

Jackeé, 92

Brad Johnson, 21, 22

Stacy Keach, 42

Gene Kelly, 65

George Kennedy, 49

Gladys Knight and the Pips, 142

Lorenzo Lamas, 125

Diane Lane, 82

John Larroquette, 89

Ronnie Laws, 37

Peggy Lee, 48

Janet Leigh, 109

Jay Leno, 23, 140, 141

David Letterman, 141

Judith Light, 57

Hal Linden, 53

Sophia Loren, H, 11, 12, 36, 121, 133

Susan Lucci, 75, 76

Ali MacGraw, 134

Lee Majors, 26, 135

Ed Marinaro, 14

Johnny Mathis, 128

Mitzi McCall, 52

Alyssa Milano, 20

Nolan Miller, 118

Donna Mills, 41

Ricardo Montalban, 108

Dudley Moore, 129

Pat Morita, 140

Paul Newman, 28

Wayne Newton, 45

Michael Pare, 17

Valerie Perrine, 138

Victoria Principal, 5, 6, 7

Sheryl Lee Ralph, 63

Ahmad Rashad, 154

Phylicia Rashad, 154

Don Rickles, 48

Kenny Rogers, 46

Wayne Rogers, 104

Jane Russell, 109

Pat Sajak, 62

Jack Scalia, 18, 103, 130

John Schneider, 105

Jane Seymour, 19, 111

William Shatner, 64

Cybill Shepherd, 24

Kathy Smith, 95, 96, 97, 98

Robert Stack, 56, 77

Rosemarie Stack, 77

Danielle Steel, 100

David Steinberg, 122

Jill St. John, 79, 144

Elizabeth Taylor, I, 1, 35, 50, 116, 117, 149

John Traina, 100

Ted Turner, 152

Bob Uecker, 68

Blair Underwood, 13

Robert Urich, 147

Vanity, 33, 34

Ben Vereen, 3

Jan Michael Vincent, 127

Robert Wagner, I, 78, 79, 145

Katie Wagner, 78

Gene Wilder, 139

Wilhelmina, 114

Billy Dee Williams, 81

Paul Williams, 143

Bruce Willis, 24

Natalie Wood, 55, 90

Kay Sutton York, 15, 51, 86, 87, 124

Stephanie Zimbalist, 70

1. ELIZABETH TAYLOR, *Los Angeles, 1989*

# FOREWORD

by Elizabeth Taylor

It is said that each artist chooses his tools.  The painter uses his brush, the potter uses his hands, the sculptor uses his hammer and chisel.

Gary Bernstein uses his eye.

Gary's eye sees what his camera captures:  The very substance of his subject.  No matter how transcendent that element is—no matter how strong, how fleeting or how beguiling—he captures in the still moment the legends of our lifetime and how we best want to remember them.

Anyone can operate a camera; it takes someone with a gift as special as Gary's to see the essence of legend.

Thank you, Gary, for some of the most memorable photographs I have ever known.

Elizabeth Taylor
Bel Air, 1994

# INTRODUCTION

by Monte Zucker

Hollywood's legends have the power to dazzle the eye, kindle the imagination and swell the heart with passion and romance. It is this power that elevates a celebrity's flesh and blood into larger-than-life fantasy. Gary Bernstein lives in that fantasy world, and now he shares it with us all.

What is it that makes being in a celebrity's company the ultimate dream? Is it their faces? Their distinctive features? Their larger-than-life essence? Whatever it is, Gary finds that magic and captures it in his photographs. Every Bernstein image in *Portrait Hollywood* is a singular work of art . . . living, breathing and glowing with stunning detail.

Bernstein has a special talent for visualizing and capturing each of his subjects in a grand manner with seemingly little effort. His straightforward studies capture not only his subjects' outward beauty but also their inner being . . . the force driving their intellect, the flame lighting their passion.

Hollywood's photographers live on the edge. Gary thrives in this environment because his vision, instincts and experience have taught him to watch and wait for that one incredible moment. It's then that the payoff comes—for the artist, the subject and the viewer.

He seems to photograph for fun and loves to experiment. He gives each of his portraits an elegance and excitement that captures the eye and the imagination. Every photograph that Gary creates is striking in realism, or quiet and subtle when delicacy is required.

Gary is one of the finest photographic artists of our time. We have been great friends for many years and I am thrilled to have been an influence in his young developmental years as a portrait photographer.

For sheer elegance, no one can touch the talent of Gary Bernstein. No wonder, then, that Hollywood—the most magical of places—has elected Gary to be its special friend, the one it trusts to lock into eternity those special moments of perfect beauty and dynamic power.

Monte Zucker
Silver Spring, Md., 1994

# PREFACE

by Gary Bernstein

I fell in love with photography at an early age and enjoyed every aspect of the art from the production of still lifes to landscapes. But it was only in making pictures of people—seeing the pleasure on their faces when they saw the results—that photography became more than a personal art. It became a relationship.

The biggest step in any professional photographer's life is leaving amateur status—a move from complete artistic freedom to art for hire. This is just simple reality. Consequently, when I turned pro, I needed to find a center, a foundation from which any portrait would retain its integrity regardless of its ultimate use.

My theory was simple: To please the subject with his or her own image and depict the beauty and strength I saw. My subject has always been paramount. So in these images, you stand with me in that dedication and see with my eyes. And in the eyes of every subject contained here, you see the reality of our brief relationship at a unique, singular moment in time.

It's not easy being the subject of a still photograph. It usually requires an emotional adjustment. I've watched my closest friend become a complete stranger, taking on a totally different air from the moment I pointed a camera in his direction. This is perfectly understandable, as we all want to be recorded in a complimentary way and by our own standards. Looking into that lens can make anyone self-conscious. Accepting that, it shouldn't be surprising that even the most celebrated actors may experience the same feelings in a photography session. It's my responsibility to ease that burden and make the camera disappear so that nothing interferes with the honesty of our relationship.

☆     ☆     ☆

Rock Hudson was a friend long before he agreed to pose for me. A wonderfully genuine man of grand stature (he stood 6-foot-6) with great warmth and a tremendous sense of humor, Rock's real-life presence was as if he had just stepped off the big screen. Yet he expressed to me his great discomfort in front of the still camera. As an actor, he felt that his concentration centered around his character and the emotions required by the script, as opposed to what he described as the inescapable coldness of the still camera.

"I can move and emote in front of the motion picture camera," he said, "but here, I feel confined. It's so static."

When I shoot, I like to light the subject first and then make subtle adjustments throughout the session. Rock preferred not to work that way. He asked if he could turn away from me between shots and come back to the camera with a different "attitude" each time.

We tried his approach but we agreed it still wasn't working.

"Rock, just look at me. Let me work with you on the shot," I suggested.

He replied that the only way that approach would work was if I did something to make him forget he was being photographed. At that point, I broke into my worst rendition of "Melancholy Baby."

I began to shoot, singing at the same time. Slowly, Rock's face changed from grim and stern to bright and cheerful.

Although his time with us was dwindling when the images that appear in *Portrait Hollywood* were made, hopefully they capture the essence and aura of Rock Hudson as the world knew him.

**A, B, C, D. ROCK HUDSON,** *Culver City, 1984*

My best form of advertising has always been word-of-mouth, and I was absolutely thrilled when I heard that Natalie Wood wanted me to photograph her.

At the time, I was shooting for Avon, Faberge and Revlon as well as the New York fashion magazines. When I was hired to shoot a major celebrity campaign, I thought Natalie Wood—whom I had long wanted to photograph—would be perfect, so I contacted her publicist.

I met Natalie a week later at her home, an elegant, understated, French-country estate in Beverly Hills. We discussed the photography session, which would consist of the advertising shots I needed and the personal public relations images Natalie wanted. After selecting the wardrobe and setting the time for the shoot, I picked her up a few days later and took her to my Los Angeles studio for the session.

Natalie was sweet and beautiful with a childlike innocence. She was one of the first celebrities I had worked with and I was taken aback by her complete trust in my taste and judgment. She knew how much I wanted her to be pleased with the results.

Within those eyes—the darkest eyes I've ever seen—there was a rare grace and sincerity. Although I never had the opportunity to photograph her again, the memories of that session remain remarkably clear.

☆　　☆　　☆

I prepare extensively for private and commercial photography sessions. Celebrity commercial shoots are the most involved because, technically, I have two clients: the celebrity and the advertiser. Once I've met with the art director, gone over the layouts, scheduled the appropriate stylists and constructed the needed sets, I'm able to allow the spontaneity of the session and my interaction with the subject to take over.

My session with Robert Duvall was different. I had very specific pictorial desires influenced by the amazing range of his acting talents. I wanted to combine the sensitivity of his character in *The Godfather* with his unnerving intensity in *Apocalypse Now*.

The session took place in the Fifth Avenue penthouse of designer Jean-Paul Germain. Duvall was in the middle of rehearsals for a play and could give me only an hour of his time. He spoke of nothing but acting from the time he entered the room. I asked him to go through a range of emotions as we shot—that he become some of the favorite characters he had played—while working to the camera. He enjoyed being directed. Sometimes it takes a while for the subject to get into the session, but Duvall's images were strong from the beginning.

Toward the end of the hour, I asked him if, when he read the *Apocalypse Now* script, he envisioned the impact of his now-classic line—one of the most famous film lines since Gable's "Frankly, my dear . . . "

He responded by asking if I'd like to hear him deliver that line. Never one to turn down a gift—and certainly not one so precious—I said yes.

"I love the smell of napalm in the morning," he sneered. "It smells like victory!"

So did our session.

☆　　☆　　☆

I owe a great debt—as does all of Hollywood, for that matter—to Nolan Miller. Miller, the television and motion picture industry's most celebrated designer—whose elegant fashions appear throughout this volume—helped me realize one of the great ambitions of my career: to photograph Sophia Loren.

This desire simmered for nearly a quarter-century; while presumably studying architecture in Florence, Italy as part of my undergraduate studies at Penn State University, I actually spent more time trying to book a photographic session with Sophia. My efforts were never successful.

Years later I was at Nolan Miller's studio and noticed—among designs for Elizabeth Taylor, Joan Collins, Lana Turner and other members of Hollywood's elite—a new gown for Sophia Loren. I told Nolan of my long-standing desire to photograph "Italy's Greatest Treasure."

A few weeks later, Nolan called and said, "Gary, there's a beautiful woman here I think you'd like to speak to." On the other end was Sophia Loren.

I hopped in my car and raced to Nolan's studio where I met Sophia, and we arranged the session for the following week at my studio.

The session was indeed worth the wait. Sophia is a woman whose awesome beauty is surpassed only by her kindness, sensuality and earthiness. We shot all day, during which we went through a half-dozen wardrobe, set and hair changes.

Photographically, Sophia works the still camera as if it were the ciné camera: She moves slowly and deliberately, displaying a range of emotions from the most heart-swelling happiness and laughter to the deepest sorrow. At one point she displayed a depth of emotion that was breathtaking to photograph. Later I asked her, "Sophia, what was it that made you show such sadness?"

"Some days are happy," she said in her beautiful Italian accent, "and some days are sad. I remember them all."

Interestingly, although willing to display the great depth of sadness for the camera, she didn't select any of those images for use and they remain unprinted to this day.

☆     ☆     ☆

In addition to word of mouth, media and publication credits have been responsible for the majority of my celebrity associations. In one special case, it was divine providence and bad driving.

While driving home about 15 years ago, I was nearly blindsided and hit by a guy who had run a stop sign. Putting it mildly, I was upset. I gave chase, fully intending to show him my extreme displeasure. I caught up with him, got out of my car and challenged him to get out of his. When he locked his doors, I became further enraged. My tantrum was interrupted when another car approached and stopped behind me. I heard a lovely, lilting voice in a classic English accent say, "My, my, haven't we a temper?" I turned around and saw Joan Collins, a wisp of a smile on her face, sitting in the back seat of a limousine.

Instantly recognizing legendary Joan, I told her I was a photographer and handed her my business card before her driver sped away—which, incidentally, the guy I had cornered had already done.

Years later, I was booked to shoot the advertising campaign for the ABC show *Dynasty*. I had worked with John Forsythe before, but had never shot with Joan, who was to be featured with John in the photographs. As my assistants began setting up the lights, John and I were talking when Joan walked in. John called her over to introduce us and I mentioned to her that, although she probably wouldn't remember, we had met briefly years before.

To which she replied, "I saved a poor guy's life in Beverly Hills and you don't think I remember?"

Since then, Joan and I have worked together countless times. With successful careers in acting, writing and merchandising, she is as busy as any celebrity I work with. As a result, our shoots are always time-constrained, yet this celebrated beauty and sex symbol always brings a lightness and levity to a session that mitigates the pressure. She has natural abilities as a model; I know she can feel the "weight of light" on her face—an attribute usually reserved for top models. She is truly the ultimate professional, and every time we work together the images get better. That's as it should be.

**H. SOPHIA LOREN**
*Culver City, 1994*

☆     ☆     ☆

I had the opportunity to photograph Peter Fonda—the hero of an entire generation during my college years—a few days before his father, Henry Fonda, passed away. We were dealing with time constraints for an ad campaign and couldn't reschedule the session which, understandably, had to be brief.

Prior to Peter's arrival, I guessed at the lighting and had it set. Additionally, I selected only one generic background I'd use for the entire session.

Sometimes my greatest energy is spent hastening desired mood changes in the subject. Other times I simply go with what is there. On this day, Peter's saddened emotional state was evident from the time he entered the studio. He spoke quite candidly of his personal feelings, his relationship with his family and his feelings about his father. His words seemed to serve as a personal catharsis. Although he tried to muster a lighter attitude in many of the photographs, his heart was just too heavy. The eyes truly are the portals of the soul, and I believe the reality of the moment is reflected in Peter's portrait.

☆     ☆     ☆

The Johnny Carson seen by millions on the *Tonight Show* is the same Johnny Carson I've had the pleasure to work with. The wonderful personality, the dry wit, his amazing sense of timing and the inherent humility America fell in love with is ever-present in this special man. I usually photographed Johnny for fashion advertisements and we always had more to shoot than time would allow. Many times he has saved an overly tense session with a perfectly timed punch line.

During one of our shoots when his look and body language was abundant with classic Carson mannerisms, I said, "John, half the time I'm photographing you, I get the feeling you're doing an impression of Johnny Carson."

"Would you rather see Ed Sullivan?" he asked, doing an amazing impression of Ed. I quickly preserved Johnny's Sullivan on film.

"Or how about Humphrey Bogart?" Johnny proceeded with an impeccable Bogey impression. Again I captured the moment on film.

"Johnny," I said, "I think I'd prefer just the devilishly handsome Carsoni." Immediately, he launched into a cavalcade of funny faces, with my camera capturing every change in expression (and thank God for motorized cameras).

To this day, whenever Johnny leaves a message on my answering machine, my first thought is, "OK, who's the wise guy doing an impression of Johnny Carson?"

**E, F, G. JOHNNY CARSON,** *Malibu, 1983*

**I. ELIZABETH TAYLOR and ROBERT WAGNER**
*Hollywood, 1986*

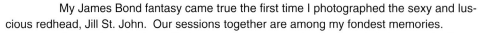

My James Bond fantasy came true the first time I photographed the sexy and luscious redhead, Jill St. John. Our sessions together are among my fondest memories.

Once, she asked me, "Is there anything more elegant than R.J. in a tuxedo?" It was a rhetorical question. Robert Wagner doesn't need a tuxedo to be elegant.

The consummate actor, Wagner is as genuine and wonderful as his years of screen artistry would lead his fans to believe.

When R.J. invited me to lunch on the set of *There Must Be a Pony* in June 1986, I knew it was for more than his timeless jokes and fine food. "You know that classic image you made of Natalie?" he asked me. "I want you to make some classic images of me and my leading lady."

With appropriate suspense, he revealed that his leading lady was none other than Elizabeth Taylor. I didn't have the opportunity to meet Elizabeth that day, but from the moment her name was mentioned my imagination raced with pictorial visions of R.J. and Elizabeth together.

There is tremendous pressure in this business but I never felt more pressure than the days leading up to the shoot. Sessions with Wagner are always easy. His humor and enveloping zest for life quickly eliminate the pressures of a commercial shoot. As we say in the martial arts, Wagner is "centered." But I had never photographed Elizabeth before, and the prospect of photographing the two legends together—particularly in light of the many pictorial requirements of the session—played havoc with my nervous system.

It was very hot the day of the shoot, and as luck would have it, the air conditioning in my studio broke. At the last minute I had to secure a rental studio in Hollywood, greatly adding to the pressure.

Elizabeth entered the studio, filling it with her indescribable aura and her wonderful, rich, warm laughter. There's a lilt to Elizabeth's walk and the way she moves that is pure royalty. I was taken by her youthfulness; she is truly ageless. When I looked into those very special eyes, I saw a melding of so many different characters, from the young girl in *National Velvet* to the temptress in *Butterfield 8*. She works the camera magnificently, and I believe our first session did indeed produce some classic images. How could I miss with my two subjects?

Elizabeth and I have shot together countless times since that first session. The pictures I've made of her over the years are among my very favorites.

☆     ☆     ☆

*Portrait Hollywood* encases my 30-year passion for photography and my life in a world of beauty and glamour.

The images in this book were originally produced for a variety of purposes. More often than not, they were for magazine, fashion or advertising clients. Sometimes they were for the individual subject's personal or public relations use. In other cases, they were strictly for me.

Mine truly is fantasy work. But my work is also commercial photography with all its big-business trappings. Consequently, it's good for the soul to step back periodically and create art just for the sake of art. I am fortunate to have been blessed with a source of constant vitality by the presence of one unique individual in my life: my wife, Kay Sutton York.

Our life together began when I moved from Washington, D.C., to set up my first New York City studio. I had long been a fan of Kay's—a top model with the Ford Agency in New York—although we had never met. As I sat in my new studio fantasizing about my rise to the top of New York's photography ladder, Kay's image was always on the other side of the lens. My fantasy soon became a reality.

Kay had been selected as the model to launch a major perfume campaign and the client was testing three photographers. Two were well-established New York pros; I was the upstart. In fact, I had gotten the opportunity to test for the job by literally pleading my case directly to the client, who apparently admired my tenacity.

As I looked through my lens at Kay for the first time during that test, I had never seen anybody as exquisite and beautiful. I fell in love with her during that shoot. Since our first session, we've shot an endless list of commercial accounts together. Our favorite photographs, however, are those we produce for the sheer joy of it. Kay was the sole subject in my first book, *Burning Cold*. To this day, when my photographic energies need recharging, when the pressures of the commercial world make me weary, Kay and I head for the studio. Because of her, I am not in need of lengthy sabbaticals.

Gary Bernstein
Beverly Hills, 1994

2. ROBERT DUVALL
*New York, 1981*

3. BEN VEREEN
*Los Angeles, 1979*

4. JOAN COLLINS
*Culver City, 1993*

5, 6, 7.
**VICTORIA PRINCIPAL**
*Culver City, 1989*

8. LARRY HAGMAN
*Dallas, 1983*

**11, 12. SOPHIA LOREN**
*Culver City, 1994*

14. ED MARINARO
*Culver City, 1983*

15. KAY SUTTON YORK
*Aruba, Netherlands Antilles, 1976*

16. NANCY ALLEN
*Culver City, 1990*

**17. MICHAEL PARE**
*Beverly Hills, 1984*

18. JACK SCALIA
*Culver City, 1988*

19. JANE SEYMOUR
*Encino, 1990*

20. ALYSSA MILANO
*Hollywood, 1989*

21, 22. BRAD JOHNSON
*Culver City, 1988*

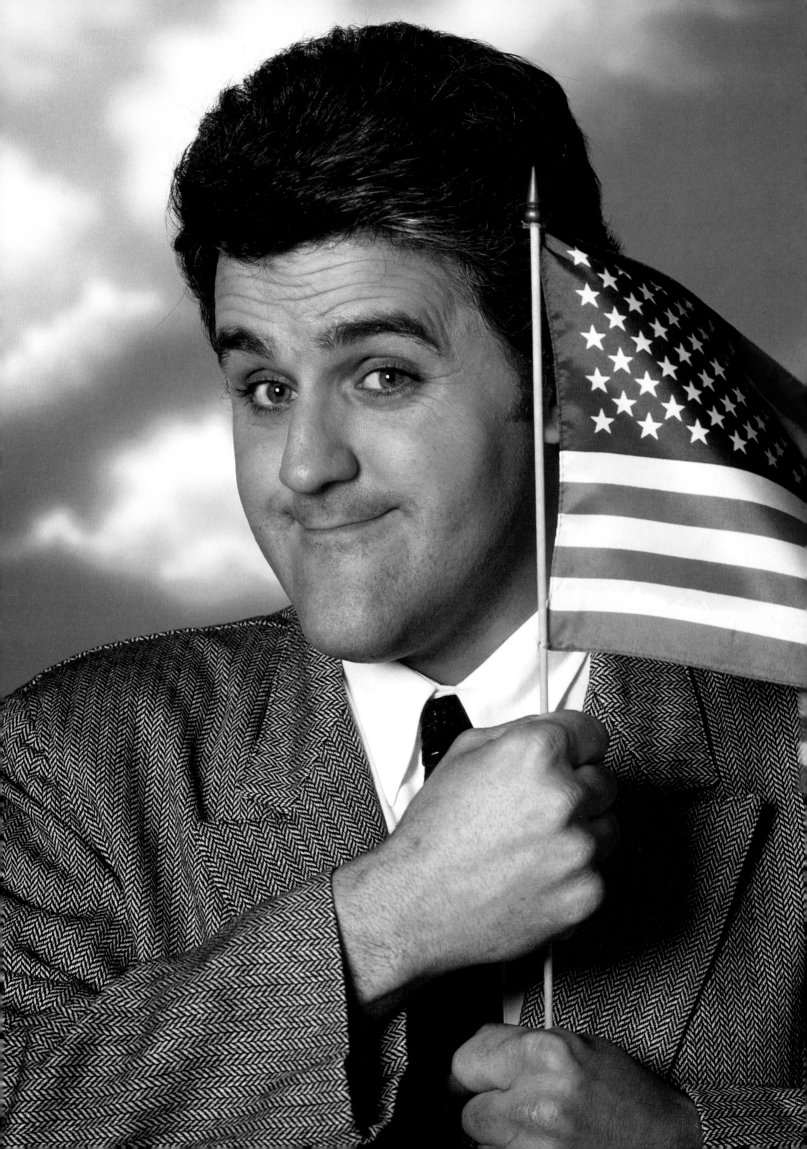

**24. CYBILL SHEPHERD,
BRUCE WILLIS**
*Culver City, 1985*

**23. JAY LENO**
*Culver City, 1987*

28. PAUL NEWMAN
*Harper's Ferry, W. Va., 1973*

30. CHRISTOPHER ATKINS
*Los Angeles, 1982*

31. CHEVY CHASE
*Culver City, 1983*

**32. JOAN COLLINS**
*Culver City, 1994*

33. VANITY
*Culver City, 1988*

**35. ELIZABETH TAYLOR**
*Hollywood, 1986*

**37. RONNIE LAWS**
*Los Angeles, 1981*

**38. MARGAUX HEMINGWAY,
UVA HARDEN**
*New York, 1975*

**39. DYAN CANNON**
*Culver City, 1992*

40. ELLIOTT GOULD
*Los Angeles, 1982*

41. DONNA MILLS
*Culver City, 1984*

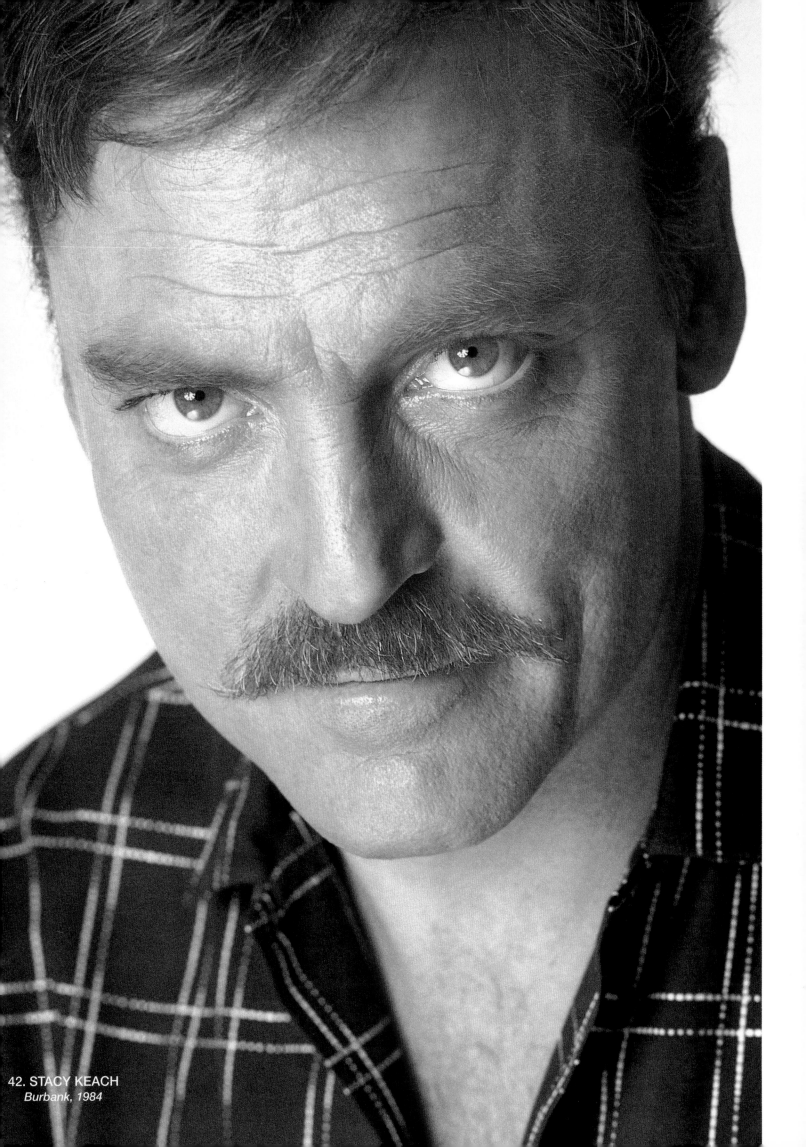

42. STACY KEACH
*Burbank, 1984*

**43. KATHERINE HELMOND**
*Hollywood, 1986*

**44. SONNY and CHER**
*Shady Grove, Md., 1972*

45. WAYNE NEWTON
*Culver City, 1994*

46. KENNY ROGERS
*Burbank, 1980*

**48. DON RICKLES, PEGGY LEE**
*Shady Grove, Md., 1971*

**47. NATALIE COLE**
*Hollywood, 1980*

**50. ELIZABETH TAYLOR**
*Hollywood, 1988*
(mixed media)

**49. GEORGE KENNEDY**
*Culver City, 1983*

51. KAY SUTTON YORK
*Beverly Hills, 1983*

52. CHARLIE BRILL, MITZI McCALL
*Culver City, 1992*

**53. HAL LINDEN**
*Los Angeles, 1980*

**54. CORBIN BERNSEN**
*Culver City, 1989*

55. NATALIE WOOD
*Los Angeles, 1979*

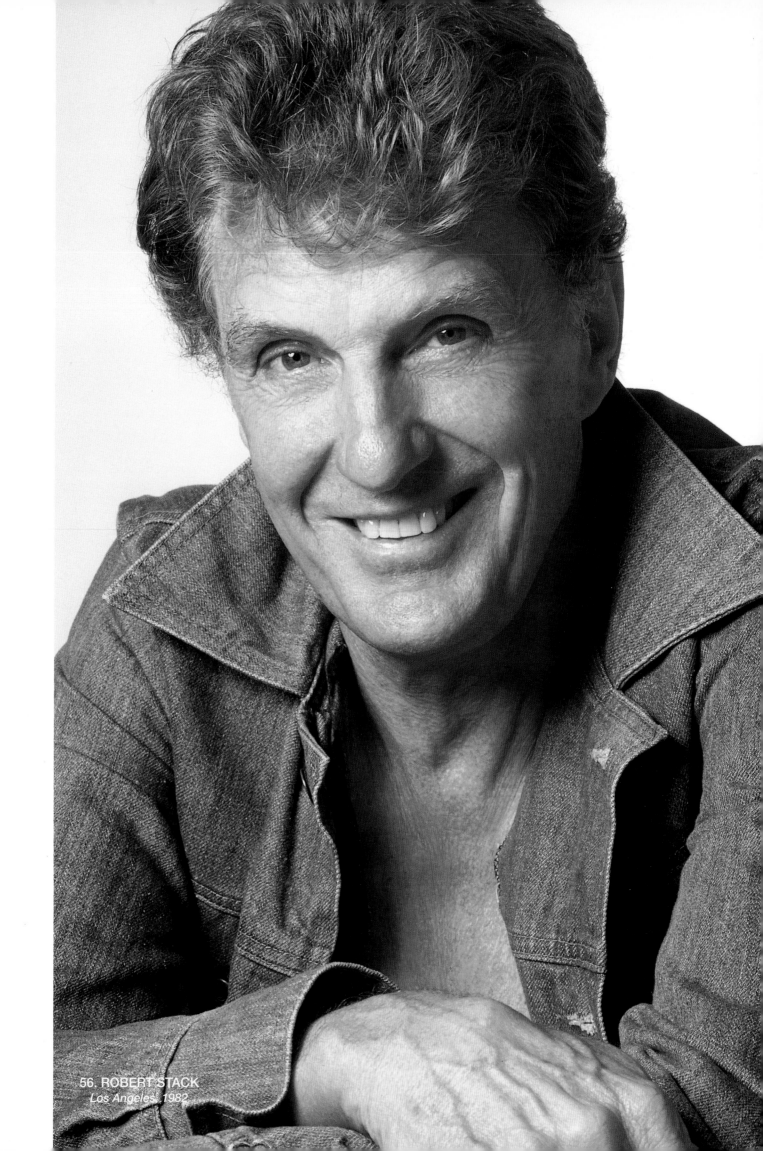

56. ROBERT STACK
*Los Angeles, 1982*

**60. MAUD ADAMS**
*Culver City, 1984*

**62. PAT SAJAK**
*Culver City, 1991*

**63. SHERYL LEE RALPH**
*Culver City, 1987*

**64. WILLIAM SHATNER**
*Los Angeles, 1982*

**65. GENE KELLY**
*Beverly Hills, 1981*

**67. ANNA MARIA HORDESFORD**
*Culver City, 1987*

**66. CHRISTOPHER HEWITT**
*Century City, 1987*

**69. NEIL PATRICK HARRIS**
*Culver City, 1990*

**70. STEPHANIE ZIMBALIST**
*Los Angeles, 1982*

**71. LORNE GREENE**
*Los Angeles, 1982*

**72. LINDA GRAY** with daughter **KEHLY**
*Culver City, 1989*

**74. LEE HORSLEY**
*Culver City, 1983*

**76. SUSAN LUCCI**
*New York, 1984*

**75. SUSAN LUCCI**
*New York, 1989*

**77. ROBERT and ROSEMARIE STACK**
*Bel Air, 1984*

**78. ROBERT WAGNER with daughter KATIE**
*Los Angeles, 1988*

**79. ROBERT WAGNER, JILL ST. JOHN**
*Culver City, 1991*

80. HERB ALPERT
*Los Angeles, 1979*

**81. BILLY DEE WILLIAMS**
*Los Angeles, 1980*

82. DIANE LANE
*Culver City, 1984*

**83. PETER FONDA**
*Los Angeles, 1982*

**84. DOUG HENNING**
*Los Angeles, 1981*

**85. RAE DAWN CHONG**
*Culver City, 1984*

**86. KAY SUTTON YORK**
*Culver City, 1984*

**87. KAY SUTTON YORK**
*Culver City, 1984*

**88. TONY DANZA**
*Culver City, 1986*

**89. JOHN LARROQUETTE**
*Culver City, 1990*

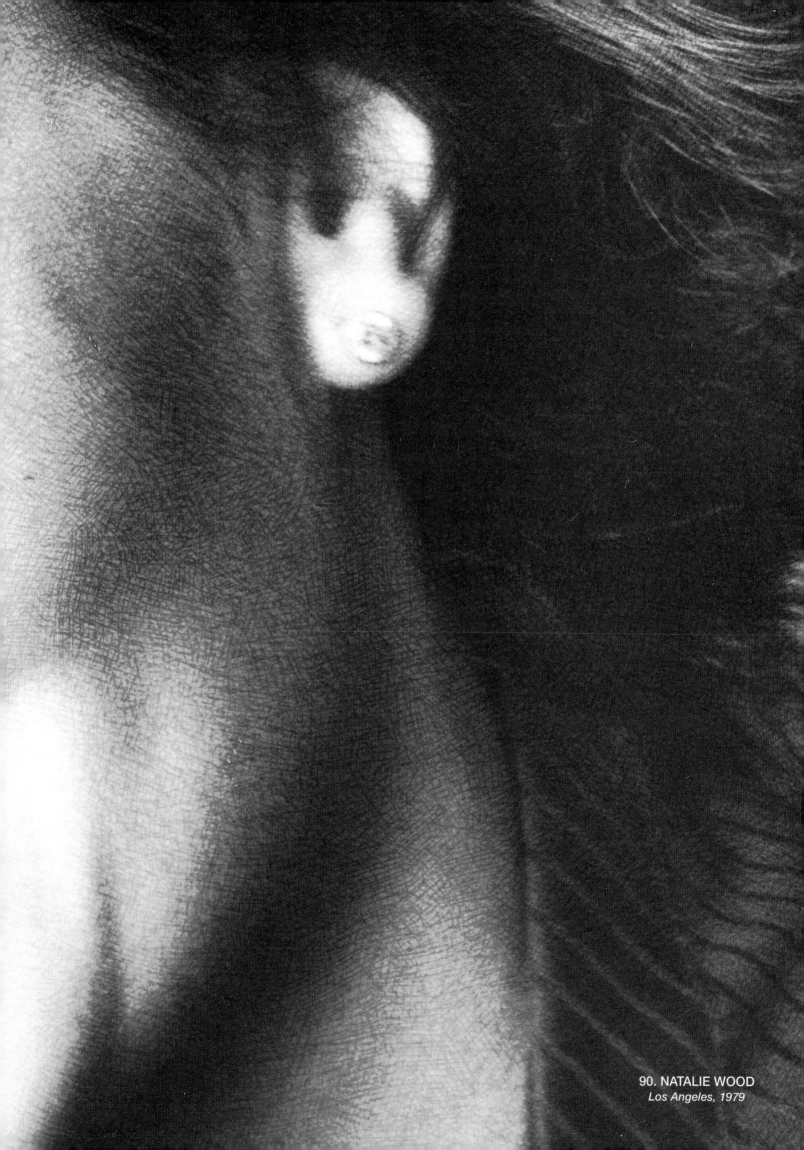

90. NATALIE WOOD
*Los Angeles, 1979*

**91. DAVID ALLEN GRIER**
*Culver City, 1992*

**93, 94. EVA GABOR**
*Beverly Hills, 1992*

95, 96, 97, 98.  KATHY SMITH
*Culver City, 1989*

99. ALEXANDER GODUNOV
*Los Angeles, 1982*

**100. DANIELLE STEEL, JOHN TRAINA**
*San Francisco, 1989*

101. JOAN COLLINS
*Culver City, 1986*

**102. JOHN FORSYTHE**
*Los Angeles, 1981*

**103. JACK SCALIA, JAY ACOVONE**
*Culver City, 1985*

**104. WAYNE ROGERS**
*Los Angeles, 1980*

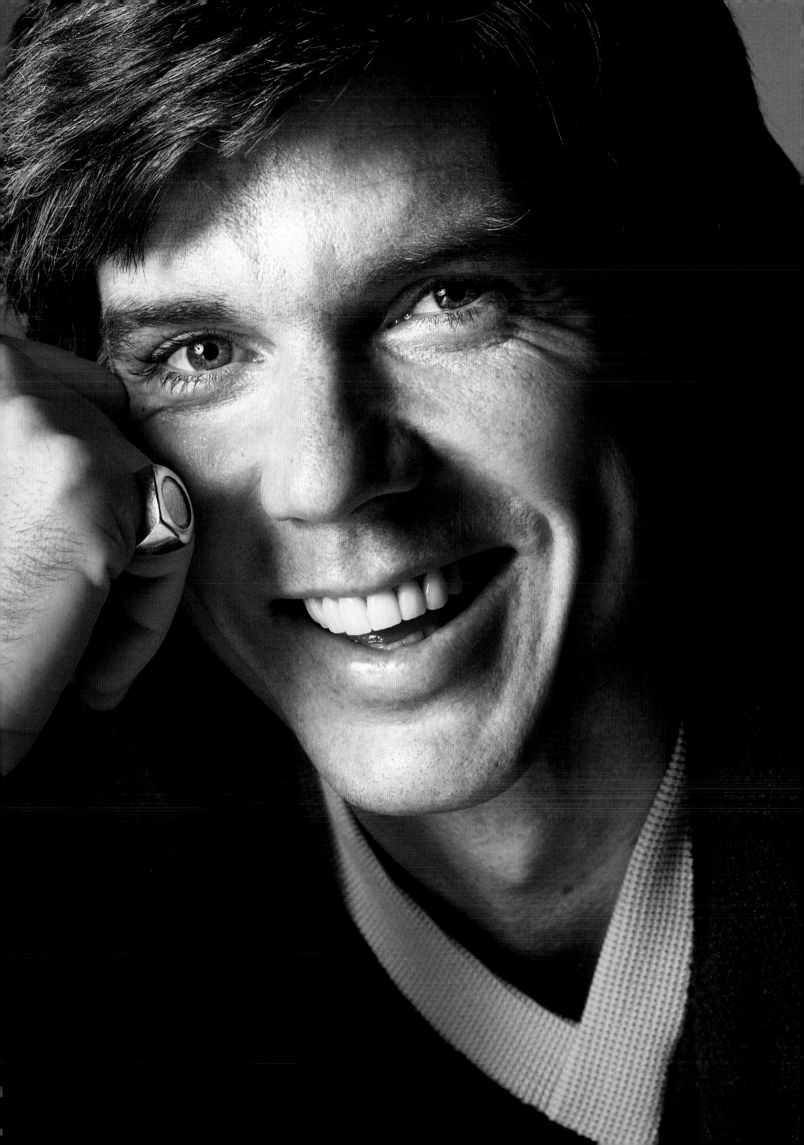

**107. MARY FRANN**
*Culver City, 1992*

**106. JOHN DAVIDSON**
*Los Angeles, 1979*

108. RICARDO MONTALBAN
*Los Angeles, 1980*

109. JANE RUSSELL, STEWART
GRANGER, JANET LEIGH
*Culver City, 1988*

**110. PAUL ANKA**
*New York, 1981*

**111. JANE SEYMOUR**
*Encino, 1990*

112. DYAN CANNON
*Culver City, 1992*

113. JOHNNY CARSON
*Malibu, 1983*

114. WILHELMINA
*New York, 1977*

115. TRUMAN CAPOTE
*Geneva, 1972*

**118. NOLAN MILLER**
*Beverly Hills, 1994*

120. TOM BERENGER
*New York, 1978*

**121. SOPHIA LOREN**
*Culver City, 1994*

**122. DAVID STEINBERG**
*Los Angeles, 1981*

**123. JOAN COLLINS**
*Culver City, 1990*
(mixed media)

**125. LORENZO LAMAS**
*Culver City, 1983*

**124. KAY SUTTON YORK**
*Beverly Hills, 1982*

**127. JAN MICHAEL VINCENT**
*Los Angeles, 1980*

130. JACK SCALIA with daughter OLIVIA
*Culver City, 1988*

**131. FRANK and KATHIE LEE GIFFORD**
*Culver City, 1992*

132. JAMES COBURN
*Los Angeles, 1981*

134. ALI MacGRAW
*Los Angeles, 1982*

135. LEE MAJORS
*Los Angeles, 1980*

**136. LINDA EVANS**
*Beverly Hills, 1988*

**137. LINDA EVANS**
*Culver City, 1987*

138. VALERIE PERRINE
*New York, 1976*

139. GENE WILDER
*Century City, 1980*

**141. JAY LENO, DAVID LETTERMAN**
*Philadelphia, 1985*

**140. JAY LENO, PAT MORITA**
*Culver City, 1987*

**145. ROBERT WAGNER**
*Culver City, 1985*
(mixed media)

**144. JILL ST. JOHN**
*Los Angeles, 1992*

146. STEPHANIE BEACHAM
*Culver City, 1989*

**148. ROCK HUDSON**
*Culver City, 1984*
(mixed media)

**149. ELIZABETH TAYLOR**
*Culver City, 1987*

**150. PATRICK DUFFY**
*Los Angeles, 1982*

**151. KATHY IRELAND**
*Culver City, 1993*

152. TED TURNER
*Culver City, 1990*

153. FARRAH FAWCETT
*Beverly Hills, 1980*

# TECHNICAL INFORMATION

W hen continually dealing with variables and often unique pictorial requirements, very few creative factors are ever a constant. But as an overview to my images, I believe that in still photography—as in quality ciné work—the technique should go unnoticed, allowing the viewer to concentrate completely on the subject. Mine is a desire to produce the highest-quality images modern film and camera technology will allow.

My use of roll film in consort with modern motorized cameras facilitates ultimate flexibility in capturing spontaneous images of people. The majority of the photographs in this book were made originally on 35mm transparency material. In certain cases where significant background information—and full-length subject rendition—was required, I photographed on 6x6 transparency material. The black-and-white images also were produced on either of these two formats.

The images were made with various lens lengths from 50mm to 180mm in the case of 35mm format; and 80mm to 150mm in the case of 6x6 format originals.

My metering and exposure system consists of taking incident readings of highlight values for transparency originals and incident readings of shadow values in the case of negative originals.

Over the course of nearly 30 years, I have used a vast quantity of equipment and services in an attempt to secure state-of-the-art rendition. Certain products, however, are a unique part of my life and my photography. I would like to give special thanks to Yashica/Contax (cameras); The Photogenic Machine Company (lighting); The Denny Manufacturing Company (backgrounds/props); Sibern International (umbrellas/reflectors); Alfa Color Labs (color prints); Spicer Hallfield (albums/photo-mounts); Quantum Instruments (battery lighting); Matthews Studio Equipment (stands and booms).

– G.B.

PHOTOGRAPH BY ROMÉ BERNSTEIN

Gary Bernstein is an internationally renowned, widely honored fashion and portrait photographer whose talents are coveted by the world's greatest celebrities and most prestigious commercial corporations. From his New York and Los Angeles studios and his Los Angeles production company, he has produced brilliant and enduring advertising, design and editorial photography for clients all over the world.

Bernstein's images have appeared in every major magazine including *Vogue, Harper's Bazaar, Ladies Home Journal, Esquire, GQ, Rolling Stone* and *Playboy.* His photographs have graced the covers of magazines such as *Good Housekeeping, Ladies Home Journal, Paris Match, People, TV Guide, Modern Photography, Playgirl, Popular Photography, Professional Photographer* and *Photographic.* He writes a monthly column for *Photographic* entitled "Pro-Talk," and his "People Photography" column appears in *Professional Photographer.* In addition, he has produced special layouts for the American and French editions of *Zoom.*

His commercial clients include Revlon, Sasson, Avon, Max Factor, ABC Television, Hart Marx, Elizabeth Arden, Dupont, Ford, Bill Blass, Nabisco, BVD, Nikon, Pentax, American Express, Pierre Cardin, SwatchWatch, Fiat Motor Cars and NBC Television.

He has photographed more than 200 international celebrities for the purposes of advertisements, editorial uses and album/CD covers. Additionally, his work has appeared on the covers of several books, including those by Rock Hudson, Danielle Steel, Kathie Lee Gifford, Joan Collins, Darryl Strawberry, Elizabeth Taylor, Victoria Principal and Maureen Reagan.

Bernstein's photographs have been displayed at the Rockefeller Center's Nikon Gallery in New York City. He has been honored as a Master of Contemporary Photography by The Smithsonian Institution in Washington, D.C. In addition, he received an honorary Master of Science from Brook's Institute in 1989 and has been honored with several awards from the Advertising Festival of New York.

Bernstein collaborated with Elton John's lyricist, Bernie Taupin, to produce the classic book *Burning Cold.* He has also authored three best-selling books on photography: *Pro Techniques of People Photography, Beauty and Glamour Photography* and *10 Secrets for Taking Dynamic Photographs.*

Shortly after Bernstein's 45-minute instructional video, *The Magic of Photography,* was released in 1986, he was selected as spokesperson for the Eastman Kodak Company and appeared in Kodak commercials and advertisements. Bernstein also has his own show, *The Bernstein Photo Studio,* on the QVC network, and divides the rest of his professional time among still photography, advertising design and film.

Bernstein was born in Washington, D.C., and has a degree in architecture from Penn State University. He lives in Beverly Hills with his wife, Kay Sutton York, and daughters Romé and Caron.

---

Co-published by:

Woodford Publishing, Inc.
660 Market Street
San Francisco, CA 94104
415: 397-1853

Waterside Productions, Inc.
2191 San Elijo Avenue
Cardiff by the Sea, CA 92207
619: 632-9190

A Tara Rose book

Woodford Publishing, Inc.:
**Laurence J. Hyman,** Publisher and Creative Director
**Jon Rochmis,** Editor
**Jim Santore,** Art Director
**Kate Hanley,** Assistant Editor
**David Lilienstein,** Marketing/Distribution Director
**Tony Khing,** National Account Executive
**Paul Durham,** Marketing Assistant

Waterside Productions, Inc.:
**William Gladstone,** President

You may order custom limited edition prints of images appearing in this book, or additional copies of the book, by writing to: Gary Bernstein Studio, 8735 Washington Boulevard, Culver City, CA 90230 or by calling Woodford Publishing, 1-800-359-3373.

Wayne

Ali MacGraw

Donna Mills

Danielle Steel

Eva Gabor

Elliott Gould

Gene Kelly

Edward Mulhare